Spreading Kindness

Being Kind at Home

by Brienna Rossiter

FOCUS READERS

PIONEER

www.focusreaders.com

Focus Readers is distributed by North Star Editions:
sales@northstareditions.com | 888-417-0195

Produced for Focus Readers by Red Line Editorial.

Photographs ©: iStockphoto, cover, 1, 8, 10, 20; Shutterstock Images, 4, 6, 13, 14, 16, 18

Library of Congress Cataloging-in-Publication Data
Names: Rossiter, Brienna, author.
Title: Being kind at home / by Brienna Rossiter.
Description: Lake Elmo, MN : Focus Readers, 2021. | Series: Spreading kindness | Includes index. | Audience: Grades 2-3
Identifiers: LCCN 2020036698 (print) | LCCN 2020036699 (ebook) | ISBN 9781644936788 (hardcover) | ISBN 9781644937143 (paperback) | ISBN 9781644937860 (pdf) | ISBN 9781644937501 (ebook)
Subjects: LCSH: Kindness--Juvenile literature. | Families--Juvenile literature.
Classification: LCC BJ1533.K5 R66 2021 (print) | LCC BJ1533.K5 (ebook) | DDC 177/.7--dc23
LC record available at https://lccn.loc.gov/2020036698
LC ebook record available at https://lccn.loc.gov/2020036699

Printed in the United States of America
Mankato, MN
012021

About the Author

Brienna Rossiter is a writer and editor who lives in Minnesota. She loves cooking food and being outside.

Table of Contents

Chapter 1

Choosing Kindness

People can have many kinds of homes. Some live in houses. Others live in apartments. But no matter where people live, they can show kindness at home.

For example, people can treat one another with **respect**. This helps everyone feel safe and welcome. To show respect, speak **politely**. And listen to what others say.

Chapter 2

Helping Out

You can help make your home a nice place to live. One way to do this is by helping with chores. Chores are jobs done around the house. Cooking and cleaning are two examples.

There are many other ways to help. You could **decorate** or **organize**. You could sort things or put them in boxes. You could also help an adult paint or fix things.

Fun Fact

Working together gets the job done faster.

Do a Chore

Think of a chore that needs to be done around your home. Are there dishes to wash? Do toys need to be picked up? Go do this chore, even if it is not your job. You can surprise the people you live with and make them happy.

Helping at Home

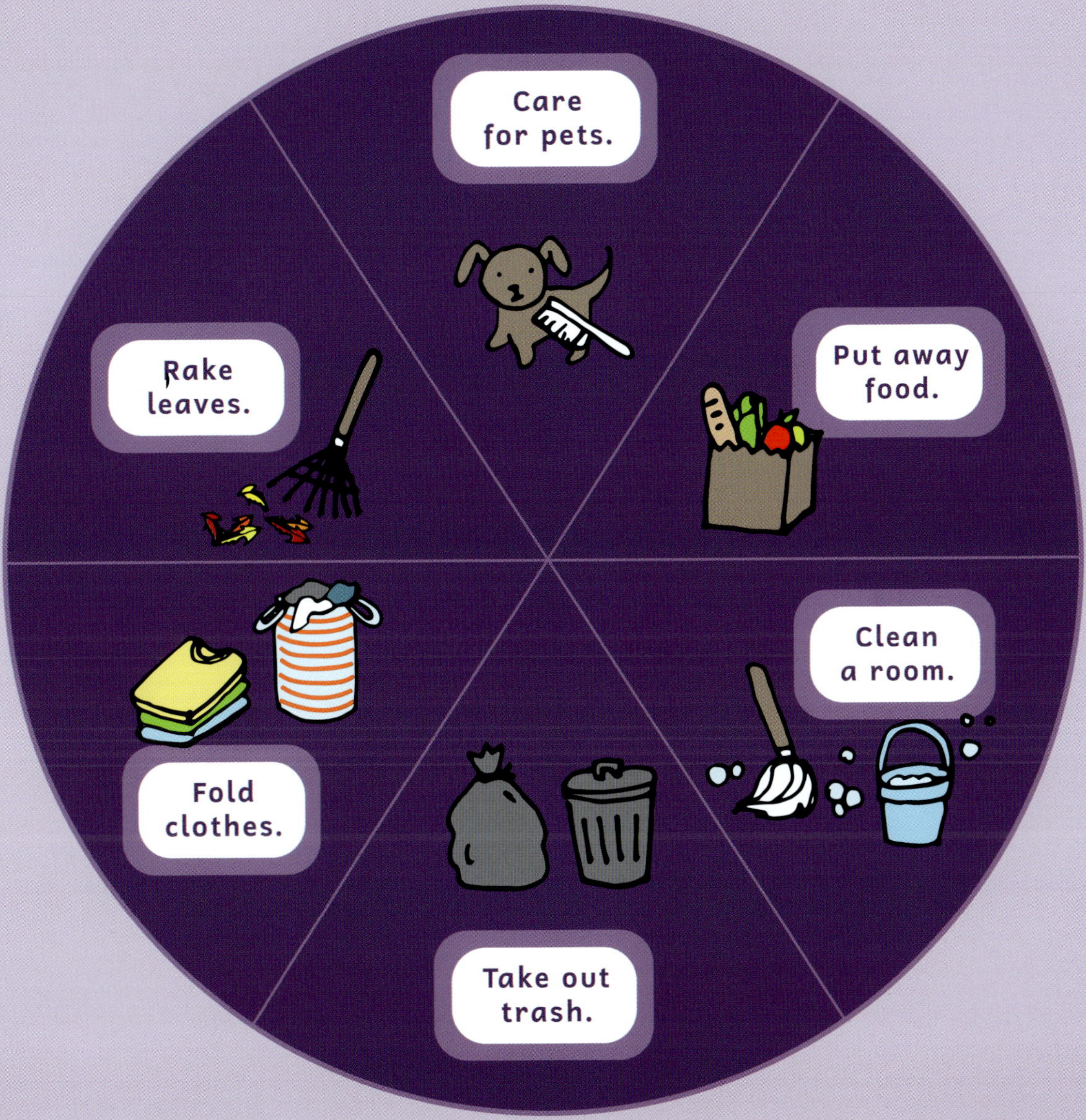

Chapter 3

Sharing

Sharing is another way to show kindness. If you have **siblings**, let them use your toys. Take turns using games. You can also take turns choosing what to do.

Families also share space. To show kindness, clean up when you make a mess. And be quiet when people are trying to sleep.

Fun Fact

Keep your voice soft when you are indoors.

Chapter 4

Time Together

People often spend lots of time together at home. It can be easy to fight or get mad. Choose to be kind instead. If you hurt someone, say you're sorry. And choose to **forgive** others.

If someone asks you to do something, don't **complain** or **argue**. Instead, go do it. This is kind to the person who asks. It shows that the person is important to you.

Fun Fact

If you feel mad, take deep breaths. This action can help you calm down.

FOCUS ON

Being Kind at Home

Write your answers on a separate piece of paper.

1. Write a sentence describing one way you can show respect for others.
2. What things are easy for you to share? When is sharing harder for you?
3. How does showing respect for others help them feel?
    A. safe and welcome
    B. hurt and mad
    C. tired or bored
4. Which is a good example of how to share space with others?
    A. making lots of loud noises
    B. cleaning up any food you spill
    C. keeping all the toys for yourself

Answer key on page 24.

Glossary

argue
To fight or disagree, especially in an angry way.

complain
To say something is unfair or say you don't like it.

decorate
To make a place or thing look nice.

forgive
To let go of your anger toward someone.

organize
To group things in a certain way, often by putting similar things together.

politely
In a way that shows good manners.

respect
Care for someone's thoughts and feelings.

siblings
Brothers or sisters.

To Learn More

BOOKS

Merk, T. M. *Journey to Joy's House: Respecting Parents.* Mankato, MN: The Child's World, 2018.

Plattner, Josh. *Manners with Family.* Minneapolis: Abdo Publishing, 2016.

NOTE TO EDUCATORS

Visit **www.focusreaders.com** to find lesson plans, activities, links, and other resources related to this title.

Index

Answer Key: 1. Answers will vary; **2.** Answers will vary; **3.** A; **4.** B